# Timely Departures

Randall Maggs

BREAKWATER

**BREAKWATER**
100 Water Street
P.O. Box 2188
St. John's, NF
A1C 6E6

*The Publisher gratefully acknowledges the financial support of the Canada Council, which has helped make this publication possible.*

*The Publisher acknowledges the financial support of the Cultural Affairs Division of the Department of Municipal and Provincial Affairs, Government of Newfoundland and Labrador, which has helped make this publication possible.*

*Cover photo: Dennis Minty*

*Author Photo: Scott Jamieson*

**Canadian Cataloguing in Publication Data**

Maggs, Randall.

   Timely departures

   (Newfoundland poetry series)
   ISBN 1-55081-108-8

   I. Title.   II. Series

   PS8576.A44T56 1994        C811'.54        C94-950155-7
   PR9199.3.M33T56 1994

Copyright © 1994 Randall Maggs

ALL RIGHTS RESERVED. No part of this work covered by copyrights hereon may be reproduced or used in any form or by any means—graphic, electronic or mechanical— without the prior written permission of the publisher. Any request for photocopying, recording, taping or information storage and retrieval systems of any part of this book shall be directed in writing to the Canadian Reprography Collective, 379 Adelaide Street West, Suite M1, Toronto, Ontario, M5W 1S5.

Printed in Canada

**In memory of my father W. J. M.**

*. . . by happening to be open once, it made*

*Enormous Alice see a wonderland*
*That waited for her in the sunshine, and,*
*Simply by being tiny, made her cry.*
　　　　　—W. H. Auden, *The Door.*

*I guess th' farther we get from Buttermilk,*
　　　*th' better, eh Sandy?*
　　　　　—Little Orphan Annie.

# Acknowledgements

Early drafts of many of these poems have appeared in *The Fiddlehead*, *The Antigonish Review*, *Grain*, *Quarry*, *Dandelion*, *The Wascana Review*, the *Newfoundland Poetry Edition* of *C. V. II* and the anthologies, *Reflections On a Hill Above a Town (Fiddlehead)*, and *Banked Fires (Cuff)*.


Thanks to Don Coles for his encouragement and sound advice, to the Banff Centre for the Arts for a place to work and financial assistance and to Catherine for the time, the most precious gift of the lot. My thanks also to Al Pittman and Nick Avis.

# CONTENTS

Land's End   7
Horses by the Bay   8
Bandit   10
Blue Murder   12
Vandals   14
The Duck-House   15
Wonder Woman Meets White Fang   16
Shy Foxes   18
My Grandfather Somewhere South of Clandonald   20
Retreat   22
Friday Night Hockey   23
The Murder-Holes   24
Guerrero: Night Falling   25
Fer de Lance   27
Tropical Toads   29
Darwin's Slow but Very Sexy Dance   31
The Road to China   33
This Dangerous Life   35
About Suffering   36
Dream-Boys   38
Horse from the South   40
Cats and Dancers   42
Berbers   44
Lights Out with the World   46
Hawks and High Places   47
Not an Aunt in Sight   49
Gundersen   50

Small Cafe   51
Providers   53
Invisible Men   54
Your Outline Above Me as Dark as the Night They Came for Your Father   55
Glass Cat   56
Atrocities and Home to Lovely Countries   57
Dog in the Gloom   59
Back at Mrs. Lund's   60
Constable's Cows   62
China Ducks   63

## LAND'S END

The sun was gone like a coin in a quick
thief's hand. The wind stopped the swoop
of gulls and drove the boats into
giddy coves. All night the sea's
boulders cracked and waves went in
to shake the stilted sheds. There and
there on the hill, curtains split showing
late lights and eyes that followed the foam as it
licked at the slope, running closer, unstacking
the day's peeled poles, swirling past the marigolds
in crenellated tires on the lawns.

Then morning and its unrepentant
sun, the bright bay, the boats
gone out again, dropped over the
scoured arc. Hours ago the cool air at
open necks, harbour chat lost in the burbling
of engines: fragments of jokes, sea-questions.
The gulls have gone but beach-birds
dash along the pounded sand, their twig legs
blurred like flipping film. They look like
silent-movie stars caught up in some comfortable
catastrophe, space invaders on the way,
a saw-blade rips toward the roped
and wide-eyed girl.

Only the manic piano's missing.

## HORSES BY THE BAY

Ponies run wild on Sable Island
and shipwrecked stallions swim for any
bit of land: still, I don't expect
this, finding horses here. One's a
pretty appaloosa, the other's grey,
squat, a solid companion. Old friends
they seem, they wait in windy grass to ask
how are things at home.

Except for them the island's
empty. Behind them blackened sawdust
humps and a mill's foundation. Were they
dreaming of apples, hoping I'd be someone else?
The appaloosa nuzzles my wrist. The grey's
more blunt and prods at my pocket.
But I've brought them nothing,
not expecting horses here.

The wind off the water goes for bone.
The grey nips at the mare, so much for
graciousness he says. I grab at
a gristly ear and jerk his head
against me, hard and scarred,
familiar as an old boot.

But I'd like to know how they ended up
here. Were they left behind when the mill
closed, like cats? Or driven across
on the ice with the woods work done?
There's a bit of meadow, a sloped and
cosy patch, but not the room that
horses want, flat ground for headlong flight,
escape routes from trouble.

Though what's to run from here?—
it's only weather on the way.
A patch of light blows into the trees
like a loose kite. Shaggy, bleak, the horses
head back to their sawdust canyons and I'm
left on the narrow beach, knowing

we've let each other down, knowing too
that, clumsy with boats and island currents,
I've got a difficult hour ahead.

These horses by the bay.
This horseman.

# BANDIT

Home between transfers that
winter, I walked with my father over
icy fields, over the gopher and bird and
outlaw bones, the litter of a bloody childhood.
A few crows fooled by the stopped creek,
black hats in the branches,
*Wasn't us*, they winked,
*Not this time. No.*

We slid down the bank surprised by
death's waspishness: how the horse lay
wrong side up, the side exposed that
living he'd always concealed,
as if the moon had rolled around,

a piebald, whose teeth we knew
but whose dark side's seas and continents
were strange. And that empty socket
he'd turned from us and
trouble, the skin pink as gum.
Un-eye. Blank.

Old Bandit. Life handed him no
flowers, got one of his eyes and
both balls but never came near what
burned inside. *That bloody Bandit,* my father
wrestled off a sodden boot, *nearly got McCambridge's
other ear.* Sometimes he'd want shelter,
bringing the herd from the hills,
*One time I look up and there's that
eye at the window,* my father sipped at
his tea, glancing over the edge of his cup.
*Melted the frost off the glass*, he said.
*Made a hole big as that pie-plate.*

The first hay was his.
The rest hung back or discovered
the order of things: the sudden crunch of
snow, the click of murderous teeth. And Bandit,

ignoring the boot that flew at his head, would lunge
at some forgetful two-year-old. Under the loft
my father hopped between the yellow, broken
puddles, not knowing what to do first
go for Bandit or his boot.

*Quick as a half-cut cat*, Dmiturko'd
say or McCambridge, someone who'd stopped
for nothing I could see, a busted
clevis maybe, something to stare at besides
the sky. Carefully, they'd watch from the fence
as he circled the others, clearing his blind side,
checking for coyotes or town-kids as close as
they'd come to Apache country. Even later,
the others dead or sold, circling
nothing in fields long since
let go to grass.

What demons you had to
wonder, what wolves or stalking
cat in his skull. Clutching at frozen
hoof prints we climbed to the moon's
meadows, looking for something loose and
convenient, something to take to
a warm kitchen: there wasn't much
but a winter afternoon,
ice-grey light,
a half-hearted razzing of crows.

## BLUE MURDER

The wind unwound in Simonette's
flax, slipped the wire, nosing
programs and paper cups like
a bored dog. Sidney and I climbed
to the last of the rump-polished planks.
Below, the silent chutes: in the scrubbed
air, an absence of whistles and slaps,
a gnawing bleakness.

The proof was clear in the makeshift
post, the fence braced where only yesterday
the brahma bull went after the crowd,
breaking his leg and his rider's,
Billy Star Blanket's;
or closer, in Sidney's eye,
black from an accidental boot.
You heard the post give way, then bone
and the bawling and thrashing about of the bull
trying to get his three good legs beneath him
and Billy his one.

And Ellie Lewis's arm popped out
again, everyone saying they seen it
fifty times and loved how the bareback
riders leapt the fence, leather chaps flying,
floating into the ring soft as
birds in a hedge, then
clumsy, running in high-heel boots
in sawdust. The crowd went wild spilling
drinks and cheering for God knows what,
the tough horse kicking and farting, ten men
trying to drive him into a corner and over it all
Ellie bellowing blue murder *Christ boys
Oh Jesus Christ boys* and someone said
*Get his arm and line her up* and they snapped it
together again. Simplest thing in the world.

*Worse than Boxing Day*, Sidney
said glumly, his eye just a slit
and a wonderful blue and we angled back

to yesterday: the shot that finished
the bull, the shouts at riders
passing below, someone letting you know
he knew them well enough to call to. Or someone
shouts *Get a good hold of her ears Curly* and
Curly, crossing his arms on his chest, shouts back,
*Hey what's this?—A Ukrainian brassiere!*
And even the women laughing and turning,
looking at one of the Texas riders.
Hard to believe they'd want to go back
to being themselves, worried over
wheat or stinkweed or kids
by the creek.

And bleakly thinking what to do,
go steal some sour plums or gather
empties, the prairie crept up and tapped us
on the shoulder:

> in the grass a blackbird whistled
>
> in Simonette's field the flax
> rolled under the sun, the small blue
> flowers like a foreign sea
>
> near the chutes a gopher popped up for
> a look, distrusting the silence.

# VANDALS

The station squats on lunar
cinders, silent, useless as a moon's
beach. Snow catches on curling boards.
Inside, the door with PASSENGERS ajar,
a match flares. There's anger here
and not-quite-sound obscenities.
Bottles pelt ARRIVALS & DEPARTURES, windmill
into the WOMEN'S. They cheer and arc their
piss across the counter, driving out green-visored
ghosts and ghosts of waiting-room drunks
keeping warm. Saturday night.
They wait all week, they wink
at lockers making plans.

Saturday night.
No moonlight glistens down
these rails. No trains to the coast
or noisy cafes, no fanfares blast the open-air
rink: you get the boos when you lose, the elbow
in the mouth, some ape from Willow Creek, grinning with
green teeth. Or gantlets thrown down, the leap of
honour, the prying prison-stripe arms. But only
five and two for roughing, never
proper terms or ropes to high windows and
sleepy arms. Only Gwennie Parker who once and
single-handedly took on the Stavely power play
beneath the stands: *Can't imagine how they beat you
every time,* she sniffs, *I wouldn't say there's
one with any wallop.*

The moon falls flat on a frozen
slough. They smoke together in the cold,
skipping rocks to the other side.

Too soon to go home on a
Saturday night.

# THE DUCK-HOUSE

Pigeon-flap and mutter, crack
of a stick: one eye opens to catch a face
in dogwood, kid-face, white as dogwood flowers.
He cocks a tape-and-plywood gun, spike for a bayonet,
door-latch for a bolt.

Above the benches a clump
of infantry, one with helmet askew, one
falling, one leaning down to urge him on to a
filmy pond in the sun, a duck-house out in the middle
a shelter from guns and dogs. Around the base,
ancient captains in spit-shone dreams, lucky
survivors of I and II and crouched behind,
a ragged ambush, the monosyllabic opponents of
God and good, whoever they happen to be
today, *crooks* or *krauts* or *gooks*.
One complains, says he hates the bloody
hiding, he's always got to take a leak. One's
in the mood for a snow-cone. One gets a leg-up,
snakes between braced and buckling legs
and fires
        knocks the white face crawling
into flowers, drags phlox and fireweed, a dead
leg, then two eyes catch the tell-tale glint
of sun: a regimental brace that startles
like a rifle in the rocks,
chinks in the gravel like a spur.

You see that exits are his
speciality, that everything has led
to this: the gun gone flying, the pitching
down to pond-muck. One arm points with the soldier
toward the pond, the swooped roof, the clever porch
with rails, the doors with red trim.
*Face down in the duck-shit*, one boy
whispers. *Jesus. Nobody dies like Frankie.*
The captains lean cautiously over their canes,
nodding. They know a good death
when they see one.

# WONDER WOMAN MEETS WHITE FANG

*Look at me Dad!! Wonder Woman!!!*
and Oh God here she comes again I can't
watch: four years old and racing down through
daisies, her blood-red cape blown out
behind. Look out for glass I want
to say, don't scrape your knees on rocks
but lean on my rake and wave a
blistered hand. I'm glad she's after evil,
but I'd rather she weren't so noisy about it or
pinned against this gun-grey sky.

And I'd sooner she were someone else.
Forget Amelia Earhart or flying females
of any sort. Madame Curie's worse—all those
germs and fumes and never out in the sun. Joan
of Arc makes me shudder: all martyr's lives
are short and messy. No doubt they're dreadful
children, reckless, preoccupied. They'd make
a father's life pure hell.

Malinche maybe. Calamity Jane in a
pinch—someone at least who'd come to terms
with compromise and grounded dreams.

But I rake what winter's left on
my lawn and bite my tongue: her crowd
wants virginal mutants, opportunistic exiles
from other galaxies, simplistic enforcers
with square jaws and shapely but
purely decorative breasts.
Ministers making the best of it,
on-the-whole good cops
won't do.

Down the hill she hurls herself,
hot for retribution. It's Cry-Baby Twist
she's after, Always-Dirty Bernice and others
whose little bums in flight I can't quite
recognize. She leaps from a rock

and shatters my hopeful
day. Her shriek stops gossip.
Dogs turn to look, three-legged.
A window falls into the street.

Oh nothing can stop her, my
marvellous daughter, mad chemists,
moats and toothy monsters, nothing but her
kryptonite, this bit of April's
dogshit on her shoe.

She hops toward me wailing,
brought so rudely into my bleaker country.
Nearby the malamute wags his tail. He's a little
uneasy, glancing at me in hopeful conspiracy.
Maybe heroes and villains can soar
to their heart's content, but
he's got to wear this
compulsory chain.

## SHY FOXES

Because she wore tight sweaters and we were
twelve, we worked at the withering gaze
in mirrors. We were noisy, deadly
with head-locks, indian burns.
Arnold Carver scratched *ten-count*
on one fist, *sudden death* on the other.
Tall, still and cool with her Icelander's
eyes, pale blue she seemed and death
to mothers. Once a week she came for
art and Arnold kept his jacket on in class,
collar turned up. Inside, his hair
thawed and stuck out like nails
under floors.

*Weasels*, she wanted, *wolves or owls*,
*winter things* and talked about the energy
of curves. Even Arnold shut up when she turned
to the board, our eyes poor moths about her,
wanting to beat ourselves senseless
against her cold white light.
Outside, the wind's ragged moan.
Snow caught in stubble.
Bored, the girls who smoked with
older boys across the road, yawned and
licked at lipstick on their teeth.

At noon we leaped the banks
and hacked out lumps
of ice for goals. Oh crafty
we were on slippery streets, clever
with shifting allegiances, smirked apologies.
Out in the wind we were dazzling: the surgical
hook from behind, the back-hand flick,
the frozen ball tucked in behind
Arnold again.

But inside, the bears and wolves in bars
of ivory soap slept soundly into
spring, shy foxes hid in snow—
*Don't hold yourself so tight*, her voice

at my ear, her hair like snow against a cold moon,
*and move like this with me.* My trapped hand
slipped, decapitating a humped and cuddly
bear, a witless, hopeless bear without
any snarl at all, the blade neatly
slicing my thumb to the bone.

The smell of soap brings back the bright
bone. Arnold gags. The girls with Egyptian
make-up moan, forgetting for a moment the shivering
boys in wind. Out in the hall with her alone,
I hated all I was and what I always wore,
those breeches my mother adored with
button-fly and suspenders. What I wanted
was jet-boots like Arnold Carver,
Cuban heels and chains.

# MY GRANDFATHER SOMEWHERE SOUTH OF CLANDONALD

I sit on the porch in the afternoon.
You see the gate from here, dust if
someone goes by.

There's an iris or two still
bloom, a dog who doesn't do much but
twitch at rabbits in his brain. A bit
cracked I always said but clever
in his own way. He still gets out
for a prowl when it's cool. I see him
where the rhubarb was, sniffing
at a stump, a little shaky
when he lifts his leg.

Somewhere on the way we made our
peace with the wind. Now we
watch as it fools in Dmiturko's oats and
listen: a piece of tarpaulin beats against the barn,
a door bangs shut in one of the sheds.
Look at him now—one time he'd be
off like a shot, scattering shadows
in forty directions.

But no one's coming, only rain.
Sometimes just before it starts there's a
stillness in the fields like after an engine's
stalled or a fanbelt's busted.
Then that smell of dust that
gets you in the knees.

And this house. A grey island in a
green sea. Dmiturko's oats to the door
in fields that once belonged to me. I could
tell you more. Sometimes there's
more: once a wolf just there by the iris
bed. Or Saturday nights, Dmiturko's boys on their
way to town. They hardly take the teams
out any more. Sometimes I listen
thinking I hear the jangling—it sounds
so clear.

And every time, he
gets me, even when I'm sure he's
sound asleep, whenever I'm straining to hear
what's there, he's watching me
with his mocking eye.

It's only me he catches now.

# RETREAT

A cot's where I sleep now
down in the kitchen. I keep things
close. My axe behind the stove, my few
tools on the table, my Swedish vice bolted
into the oil-cloth and oak, though what's an
old man need to grip tight except himself.
At night that knocking on the walls that
starts the letting go, my mind
letting go like ice in spring.

Sometimes I know it's only a shaky
limb. Sometimes like a kid in a crazy
dream, I want to stamp my feet and bellow,
scare the bejesus out of whatever's
up there. But my legs won't work
and I can't speak.

I open the vice and crank it shut,
the movement smooth as ever. I know it
better than this wrinkled hand.

A book or something falls and something
scrabbles across the floor—wouldn't Ellen jump?
Then, so clear, it's her above the stairs.
*There's horses coming*, she says.
*Simonettes*, I say. I know
the ring of their team. That weld's
let go or their cows in my fields again.
They'll stop for a bit, that bread
she's baking smells done.

Always there's part of me saying *don't fall
for this there's nothing there.*

Who's having fun with who I'd
like to know.

# FRIDAY NIGHT HOCKEY

I'm home late from hockey and the lengthening
after, the not-quite-satisfying drinks,
the talk of who was slick tonight;
*last call*, then the ABC Cafe: egg rolls
on cardboard, plastic forks and pay in advance.

Even the dog's asleep. I find
the box by the door, my daughter's printed
note attached: *For the people poor*.
Like spider's legs her crickly letters.

Inside, all her jewelry: old pendants,
earrings, a sword dancing pin, her treasure from
attics and slightly batty aunts. And I
think of her scrunched-up silence
after the story, after the Prince's gift
to the poor: the tearful swallow's peeled away
the golden skin, pecked out the sapphire
eyes. So here's her golden skin left
in trust to some night-tripper who
knows the narrow darker streets in town,
the *people poor* in her kingdom.

I lean against the warped door so
the latch clicks. I forget the aches,
the passed pucks that get lost in my
skates, the glasses that fog.
Something doesn't want to be
disturbed here, the dog's perfect dream,
the porch's dimensions, its irises in green
and silver jars. Everything stops and holds
firm for a moment, though there's
work to be done before morning.

# THE MURDER-HOLES

Above the town in cloud what's
left of a castle, little more than walls
and a moat. The draw-bridge is down, awaiting
the wheels on stone, Louis and Antoinette,
who kept to the back roads, coming
east from Paris.

The castle's rank with decay, the moat's
grass-choked. Still, there's a mood
of expectancy: a crow keeps watch
on the steep approach, cows
from the ditch and, further down,
a boy who's come to drive them home.

The evening's damp. I take
my time going up, no fishwives after me.
How many times she must have imagined the drop
to the ramp and the cautious passage across.
A little past midnight they'd said,
barring further delay. And then that mix-up
at the last exchange, the horses left at the wrong
inn. And the coach so heavy and slow.
Wavering loyalties on the way.

And only there, east
and a little south, the tempting
Rhine: how long ago that crossing into France
and the *salle de remise.* And after Schoenbrunn's
homely court, Versailles: a brothel, an open
market, you watched where you walked, cows
brought in to be milked by the beds of dreaming
princesses. Then the knives and whispers.
The listeners in corridors. You watched where you
walked. Worst of all, the pamphlets and plays,
*Je n'ai jamais été mieux fourtue* . . . .
If you've any pride you play the part
they create. And Paris mobs—she
knew them: 132 trampled trying to catch

a first glimpse of *la Belle Antoinette* and
buried in the *Cimetière de la Madeleine*. Where later,
no effort made to prepare for the "widow Capet,"
she'd be tossed on the grass and left,
her head stuffed between her legs as
the pumpkin cart returned along its
prudent track of blood.

The crow drops down for a closer
look. The gates are open. I glance up
into the murder-holes, listening for the urgent
preparation, rocks rolled to the holes, fires built
higher. Imagine the kind of arrival, trapped
horses, skulls and armour shattered by
boulders, flesh boiled from bones.

Under the hill the cows are in for the night.
There's one cafe, Calvados to drink.

It's only a small town in a rainy
corner of the country.

## GUERRERO: NIGHT FALLING

Something about the fan's slow circling,
an inside-outness nags. I close my
book or lift my pen. Eclipse? Hawk-shadow?
But it's only the sun gone again, the day suddenly
done, spent like Spanish anger over a rough
tackle. Football's finished on the beach,
the barefoot thump an echo in my skull. Inside,
the lit black eyes in cracks, the geckos wake
noisy, hungry, eager for the dash
and snatch at the light's edge.

Once more the too-bright,
too-brief day that dumps you into
night. Not like summer further
north, chair-scraping, slow-departing days,
evening's grass-stained games, slow cows
clanking into cool fields. I'm up and
pacing, picking up books and putting
them down. I take a tall gin to the beach.
Frowsy, stooped, the palms lean down to catch
the faintest sound. Something plops
at my feet, wet, glistening: a fruit bat
eating overhead. Then, without warning,
night's a tangled net around me.

Under the palms I separate the night's
sounds. Nervous dogs. Frogs. Drums from
the beach club. I trick my fear, sniffing out
the killer's economic art, the careful
stalking the leap and lovely
crumpling. Yes.
Lucky world. Lucky thing Christ came
first, then my mother and her tough demands.

Back by my small lamp, de-fanged,
I prepare for the long trek to
morning. The geckos are quieter now,
caught up in their hunt. All around me,
the crunching of wings and bones,
the gulping of soft bodies.

# FER DE LANCE

I remember you, even here
where winter stops blood, nails water
to rock, where men who never go fifteen miles
from home except by sea or think to watch for
things like you in cracks or comfortable
sea-side grass, would turn from the
slit fish in disbelief confronted
with something like you,
your icy eyes, your
yellow ugly snout.

You're just another occupant of
dreams for them, not to be taken seriously,
like *quarks* or *escargots, ben-wa balls.*
something else from away too
foolish to talk about.

But I remember you. Trapped heat
in the orchard near *Tzin Tzun Tzan,* a wasp-sung
town. Ankle-high, the wasps as bright as sun
bore into fruit on the ground and overhead
the avocados droop like bulls' preposterous
scrotums taking me back to cooler fields, better-known
boys with dangerous, high-pitched voices and
hair-pin guns. Slit-eyed, we'd creep to the fence
and Simonette's grazing bulls, wanting the good
angle: something about those bulky
bags enraged us—

So, too late the warning, too
foreign: blown fuses in a
northern brain—not
rope I'd walked on, no slapstick
rake that leapt and whacked my shin.
I sank to the ground and glutted wasps, shouting
at a wobbly sky. What God would deal with
the likes of you?  What Shepherd coil you
underfoot, deaf and so cleverly disguised?

Not that you hadn't gotten together
before. And those pickers like angels
in white—what were they grinning at?
One less gringo to eat the earth?
One more soul for a better land?
Or, being Mexicans, someone fierce or
foolish enough to rant at God Himself?
*El hombre tiene cojones*, I imagine they nudge
one another. *Si, muy grandes huevos.*
That's gold in the poke down here.

But they were pointing at
my boot and the rip an inch from
susceptible flesh.

O yes. I remember you.

My frequent visitor.

When snow slides over the cold
road or someone flips a hose across a lawn.
When I reach for clean socks in the
back of a drawer.

# TROPICAL TOADS

They're big for toads, lumpy,
soft as baseball gloves left out
in the rain. Still, they're not so easy to
see on steps in the dark or squatting near
stopped-up drains. They'll sit for hours,
unblinking, monks in the smoky light,
unperturbed by the passing world.

Single-minded, it's *equanimitas*
they're after, toad-soul hovering somewhere
window-high but leaving the warted corpse
behind, shadows in shadows and catastrophic
for careless walkers, brooders, dreamers,
lovers going up from the beach, eye-locked
and barefoot. They're the drunk's worst
fear in the tropical night, the cause of brilliant
leaps and dodges, world-class tumbles,
torn ligaments and some wonderful
lies in the morning.

Or as lovers, they're contemplative, cautious,
eschewing the bright flame, the Italian
passion. They'll drive you mad,
pledging their constancy, croaking
all night under your balcony. And they're
deadly, the people tell you, toxic if you
eat one. You wonder what they think you
had in mind, or how they know
as loose dogs know: a dog might
sniff at a toad from behind, give
it a nudge to see what happens,
the toad might hop an inch or
two but that's about it.
He won't be worried from his dreams.

It's an odd defense in a sudden, unsubtle
country, a kind of after-the-fact retaliation.
But clearly the word's got around.
And there's something decent about it,

tidy too, knowing the one you got
was the one you wanted.

They're different from things that
creep up walls and crawl into shadows,
not so frantic to stab, sting, bite, disembowel
or suck your blood. They're a lovely kind
of deadly creature, tropical toads,
you can get quite foolish about them,
so long as you send your friends
ahead in the night
and forget about the moon.

# DARWIN'S SLOW BUT VERY SEXY DANCE

Halfway to the wall in his mind and something
sweet, shattered papaya, a shock of
orange in the dust, or home
and his cracked and salty wallow,
the pig grunts once,
flops down in the road.

Let them go around him.
It's too hot.

Their shops deserted, the owners
withdraw into darker, cooler rooms behind.
There's only a dog in the street,
keeping close to shadows.

I come down to the *cantina* earlier now.
I, too, give in to the sun, attuning myself to
local rhythms (*easily swayed* my northern
uncles would murmur); besides, Mexican
beer is a pleasant surprise,
the brewers Germans who sailed in
about 1945, knowing beer and
open harbours when they saw them.

The dog's at the door glancing in
at the girl uneasily. There's something
familiar about him but Mexican dogs look
much alike—whatever stirs the *mestizo*, prize
dogs and pure lines are well down the list.
They're mongrels every one.
Still, you notice there's someone's
careful hand at work here: they're cut to
fit the town, short-haired and lean, silent,
quick to decide.

Though there's little need to be
so cautious now. The town's
shut down: the air thick and sweet,
you hear the creak and tick of an ancient

fan at noon. It makes you think of
lying down, of a damp sheet across a dark
shoulder. The dog moves on as the girl
goes across to the doorway lazily
stretching her long arms. My eyes flick open
to follow: she trails her fingers across the tables
in a way that seemed so indolent,
so hostile once.

And what about those Germans after forty
years of *pulque* and *indios?* Have they
stopped their ears to the cackling
in the trees? Do they sleep
in the afternoon heat or curse and persist,
trying to get the air conditioner
going again?

## THE ROAD TO CHINA

Once my son's face turning slowly
towards me, wanting to believe my father's
stories of grizzlies, barges, gold in the clear
river. That was in the coldest winter,
the house too silent, snow in the air
into June. Only that slow
turning to hold me.

Now it's you my dark-eyed daughter,
this search for shells to send you,
like Matins, eases me into the morning,
so early the roosters are still asleep and
moated coconut husks on the sand cast
shadows as long as logs.

The black beach stops at the basalt
wall: ragged rock and jungle that
climbs to the jaguar cave.
My shadow slides over the top and the rock
disintegrates: caught sunning themselves a thousand
crabs that scrabble for channels and back into
cracks, waving their claws at my eyes.
The basalt's pocked with salt pools,
silky sided and ridged
with razor spines.

Once by a colder sea when you were
small, we found a road that ended in
grassy dunes. Kneeling, we brushed away
sand to find the pavement ran on,
sloping down, the road to
China you decided.
The wind was sharp off the ice.
Tough grass glistened in hard light.
While I read, you dug to find dragons and
sampans, you wanted that duck that got lost
on the *Yang-tze*, then gave up the frontal assault,
crawling over pulp logs, poking through
seaweed and litter.

Here where the huts squat in rampant
vines, a rooster wakes in panic.
Looking for shells, paper-thin bones,
I kneel between the basalt knives and
search these dangerous pools so fiercely
for you, I see them begin to
boil at the edges.

# THIS DANGEROUS LIFE

*Koutoubia* floats in dawn
mist. Dark birds drop to the silent
square: *Djemaa-el-fna*, Place of Destruction,
where not so long ago the Thami Al-Glaoui
spiked the heads of thieves on posts. Like us
at home when crows would come, we'd shoot one
in spring, stretch its stiffening wings in the young
corn, a downed *stuka* in British fields, a warning
to others: be wary—ruthless dwellers here.
Nonplussed, they moved to spruces by the barn
and raided gardens down the road.

Giacometti shadows gape, the first
arrivals stacking coconuts and lemons, hanging
braids of figs, onions, birds of some sort,
plucked and headless, dangling
upside-down from hooks.

The waiter brings melon and tea, nods
toward the camel-stalls where hands that float
in sunlight whisk the flies from tongues and brains.
*Delicious, my friend*, he grins, *but more
than that: ça donne du courage.*

This morning even melon's difficult, the night's
chill hurts my teeth. I retreat behind my tidy
columns, box-scores in the *Herald-Trib:*
balks and errors, earned runs, hit-by-pitch.
Pitfalls and dangers clearly defined.

Under the terrace a legless beggar
bleats. Children race from post to post
where heads once grinned and shrivelled up
like apple-dolls. Leaving, I drop the coins
deliberately, letting the waiter see I've left enough
to pay. Importantly, they glitter in the sun,
postponing my death for another day.

# ABOUT SUFFERING

Past dancers, horses, hagglers with
braced feet, the beggar hops toward me
like a furious goat.

The waiter hasn't seen him yet.
Neatly, he shifts the tray from hand
to hand. Tall glasses clink and steam.
His grin is toothy, winkish, says wolves
we are in a world of sheep. He ducks
beneath his balanced tray to wipe
the sunlight from my table.

But the beggar's got my eye,
his teeth bared too, half-crutches propelling
his torso up the steps: plant the crutches, swing
the trunk between. I think of home and
slinkies, wind-up climbing toys that
work for about a week.

Only I am trickless and inept.
Alarmed, I hope for something to break,
a spring to give out, a crutch to catch in the rug
and crank him around. I think of gentler
importuners, boys with bruised apples
or ladies out for an hour to canvass
for crippled children.

About suffering we were
always wrong. The poor were mostly
bored, we thought, with listless goats and
bleak, elusive games with sticks. Really, not so
badly off, never made to shovel snow or take
piano. For them we ate a ton of
broccoli and clotted peas—lucky for
them sometimes they lived so far away,
Africa or France. Older, we saw them altogether
differently, gentle innocents, grateful, sharing
what we sent. We'd have boxed it up and
sent it all. Instead of stamps or

baseball cards we wanted orphans,
one in every sun-split land.

So finally wisdom's on its way, snarling
toward me across the terrasse.
But what's prepared me for this
in my life? It's like Saturday morning
cartoons, the grim Tasmanian Devil after the duck—
But who's the victim here? And what to do?
Bare my throat? Ball up my fist?
Or sit like the fool I feel and splutter
and quack like that duck? Happily, the waiter
wants no subtleties or Christian dithering. Driving
the beggar down the steps with a shout he
slaps at the hump with
his damp rag

              deftly holding the tray
in his other hand, the tall elegant
glasses undisturbed.

## DREAM-BOYS

It's like you were one of those dream-boys,
Cory or Casey or Brett, soap stars or hockey stars,
the way they slow the car and press against
the glass. But it's only to show their
absent parts, elephant joints, skin
that peels like sticker-backs.

Though the one that catches your eye hasn't a
crutch or patch or missing toes. What stops you
is her curly, orange hair—whoever sent her
out here knew who'd notice that. You think
white slave for a moment, angry, somebody's
sister. You think Little Orphan Annie,
of simpler confrontations, beating your
sister to the Saturday funnies, or Annie
herself in a walk against Axel or
J. J. Shark—*I'd slit a hundred gullets
fer a crack at dough like that,* sweet desperadoes
rampant with sinister schemes but hopeless—they'd
botch it every time, get buried alive
in a well or their boat
blown out of the water,
that dress not red for nothing.

This one's got the hair, the drain-pipe
legs, the same shapeless everyday dress.
No sign of Punjab though or Sandy's maniacal
grin. Furthermore, she's blessed with
pupils, eyes a startling blue,
her rumoured benefactors dream-boys
of another sort, Vikings perhaps, who burned
their boats imagining dark-skinned women forever,
palms and African breezes, no more ragged,
icy winds forever.

But this may be what comes of rubbing
lanterns. Susceptible Northerners
inch closer to the fire. Mothers who get

the Saturday section last look for something
new to do with hamburger, then the long evening,
hockey on again. And the red-haired girl?
Whoever sent her out here probably
ate the dog or told her it was
Daddy waiting in the car.

## HORSE FROM THE SOUTH

Do they wonder what it's like to walk
with hands?  Or have to stare at
arses all day long and scuttle away from
vain, stupid horses who rear and dance in
feigned alarm?  This toilet of an earth, rotting
feet and fruit and eye-to-eye with little thieves,
nasty monkeys with dirty knobby knees who'd
grab my place by the gate given half a chance,
the morning sun against the wall,
the crowd with money still and
half-asleep. How sweet to catch one
unaware who hasn't heard how quick
I can be, how hard I can crack them
across their knees, desert-wood my
leveller's made of, sun-baked, blasted
like myself. Sweet music his howling.
His pain. His violation—what could he say
to me about violation?

Or the horse-faced women, Germans, Danes,
I see them glance away, the guarded
blankness in their eyes. In younger,
brasher girls, a half-smile: how would he
manage this and that, a man without
God knows what—

And what about God?  And having to
beg for mercy in Allah's name?
Allah who sentences me in his
infinite mercy to squat at the
edge of things where all I see is
legs, wheels and legs, human legs, those
brainless horses' legs and dogs, mangy, bitten
mongrels not with two but four, a bitter waste,
nothing but noses and legs, sniffing at
food and female smells.

Late when the crowd's at its worst,
cranky, guarding its last coins, I climb
above the square. There, where the mortar's

missing from the wall, you see the
height is right, the angle from below—
Then they stop to notice me or, walking on,
glance back. I wait. The look's a certainty.
The guarded eyes, the lovely, careful eyes
turned up to me. For Allah has his
waggish side and blessed me with
a southern prince's face.

Or perhaps that's not quite
right, the eyes below. And it's
just a bit of a dream like the other,
the horse from the south that
wakes me always in a sweat. A bit
of a joke on myself like everyone else,
the street-rats, the grinning girls, the One
above them all. Yes, the One who
watches over all. If only my leveller
could reach that high, I tell you,
you'd see some scuttling.

## CATS AND DANCERS

Tribesmen pass his name like a traveller's
charm, Berbers ill-at-ease in close cafes,
men who know the moon's routes,
the roll of horses, the slow cartwheel
of constellations.

A Berber himself, he brings his
cafe on his donkey's back each day, a nice
twist to the old ways. Jars, pots, a portable
stove. Planks to sit on. He knows the bells and
drums and stops a moment watching dancers from
the south, his country—smoke and tricks
above the crowd, mad-men, spirits the way
they leap and whirl, as if weightless,
a devil's dance: you see the sun split
rock, horses plunge over the ridge.
Someone goes into the crowd for coins.
What could you pay for such freedom?

Greased by years of use, the last plank
slips into place. Square in a square
and him at the centre. Exactly
here. A hard-won spot but a blessing
or not he couldn't say.  Here, at least,
you see the stars and smell the wind in passing
manes. (What else but devils the way they
hammer their drums?)  But here, on certain nights
you see the stars. (And if they come again to him,
a word perhaps, meant only as a friend.)
And turns to see customers waiting
and something else, a white cat by the wall,
prim, complacent, sniffing the odours
that curl and dip from his pots.

Dreamy eyes but watchful too, she
senses when it's time to go, springs
to a ledge and onto the wall, switching
her tail at earth-bound men.

The Berbers grin and nudge
one another—no cat
tonight. Or maybe it's only the timely
departure, nothing new to them. The old man
turns back to his task. Stirring a thick stew
takes two hands and both feet
firmly planted.

# BERBERS

> *With the plough enters dishonour.*
> *—old tribal proverb.*

The way like tombs or death itself these
walls say in-here, out-there.
How they work their subtle way
when you're tired of wind and emptiness,
the numbing looking for what? water? grass?
That's when you'd think of the horses pushed hard,
cities let back to the mountains' hush, small faces
wiped from pools. Were we after something?
Or running away? There was talk, always
explanations, none of which satisfied.
Best not to wonder at all in the end.
Still, sometimes we wanted a safe place,
rocks to crouch against, a chance to rest and
see if there was someone following behind.

But goat-hide's best. Or camel.
Haul it down when the grass
is gone. Walls like these don't breathe.
Touch them when the wind blows, you won't feel
God's whisper. And worse, they make us fat
and dull and slow to act. Enemies with
any brains at all would wait and joke
about us by their fires—what sort
of fools to trap themselves like this?—
And only when we stop we start
to wear the world away: the path from
door to door, the path to the pens
where horses wait.

For what? What need for
horses now?

And how to deal with the dead?
At night you hear them in the passes,
up in the melting snow.

With horses we make these foolish
games, bump each other fiercely at the goals,
curse our mounts when they swerve to
avoid the sweet collision.

But what about the dead?

These carpets that hide the walls, half-
moons and mountains and palms—they only
remind me of what we've
become. And my son a
mason's apprentice. He wants to go
down from the mountains to work in a city of
stone. My only son.

Another of God's great jokes.

Always I thought it was Him
behind us, chasing us into the glory
of His world. In motion is grace, I thought,
the way the spirit swells when the wind
turns and the horses, restless,
smell perfect places.

# LIGHTS OUT WITH THE WORLD

Dull blue, one flower by the wall,
surviving dog-sniff and trample, goat-search,
heat like an axe. I look for something else that's
soft or bright, some desert climber draped across
a wall, a bike, a Coke or Fanta sign, something
more than naked endurance. I hear Lear's raging
at his chopping daughters, his holding out
for something more than level need.
I can't see anything here but
wind, a few shut doors,
hens wanting in from the sun.

There's a love of bleakness here like
crows at home who like dead limbs
and blackened pines. A light-pole suits them
better than apple or elegant lime, harsh metallic and
hunched like them. Even late in the fading light,
you'll know they're there—you hear the tinny
scratch of claws as, awkwardly, one turns
to watch you pass below.

My thoughts return to this blue
miracle: something's tough in beauty too.
Grass pushes up through pavement. Mountain goats
manage near-perpendicular slopes. My prairie
uncles are gentle with favoured dogs or cows.
Still, who could prosper here? What hope
at the end of a day? I watch the Arab
girl who kneels and reaches for the flower,
for what I wonder, to take the pulse of some
deliverer or tear the petals to pieces?
That's what I'd do, living here,
tear them up and go back to my own
small place, lights out with the world
and goats.

But once again, the wrong eyes.
All she does is brush the dust from
brilliant cobalt petals.

# HAWKS AND HIGH PLACES

The stop's unscheduled, sheets of galvanized
wired to posts. Chickens wake me, wondering what
bus-roofs and crates are about. Outside I hear
Casselman quietly circling, stopping up
escapes. There's a few baked huts, barely
altered earth. Nothing lives here
that isn't hard and quick.

The rippled sheets remind me of crayoned,
fishless seas, the kind kids draw with regular waves
and blunt, no-nonsense boats that only go from edge
to edge. Under the shelter, a glossy crowd from
National Geographic, Berber women with goat-cheese,
fruit, things they've sewn or glued or cut from
ragged tin. Their capped teeth glitter.
They've 20 minutes with the world and
a deal with the driver to stop at
this village, not the next.

Casselman's after oranges and olives,
praise God for patience, justice, he only
wants what's fair, raises his offer
half a *dirham*. Something's rattled back, spat
like gravel, something like *empty pockets*, *empty pants.*
The others cackle. But she's missed how he circles
the sun, his eyes on the flock's edge: she's the
youngest here, half out of the shade and
furthest away. He sulks and jokes and
coaxes then shrugs and turns as if to go.
The others watch like crows in winter
trees. They know he's got her in
a corner. It's been a bad day at
the end of the line, the driver's back
and wants to go. From the bus I watch her
hands capitulate, small and coarse
as cantaloup rinds.

Far above the sand-box bus, I soar in
feathery dreams. I pluck the sun's coins to
brighten open hands. I plunge and carry off children

to better places, towns with boulevards, matinees.
I would take them to Madame Tussaud's.

20 minutes behind, the driver
cuts corners, jars me awake.
One boot casually braced, Casselman sucks
at an olive-pit, looks at me sideways.
My ears pop, coming down,
crammed with the heckling of women
and chickens roped to the roof
in their death-crates.

# NOT AN AUNT IN SIGHT

Casbah alley, knotted sticks connect
the rooftops. A dozy, comfortable
gloom, a conspiratorial light of
tree-forts or tunnels in cedar hedges where
carrots and plums were stored and Sunday vigils
kept against monsters and mothers with aunts
to visit, lobster newburg again to push around a
tricky, not-quite-clean plate.

Here in the *rue des Rêves*, good glass
and brass in the shops, smaller brothels, a fox-faced
Arab who's cut his path. Glad he's got the Bogart
hat, he tips it back to light a smoke:
*Out of my way Mohammed, I've*
*got other fish to fry.*

Squints an eye. Angles the ominous
cigarette, though the Arab only grins, beckons
for Bogart to follow into the cul-de-sac: tunnels out
of tunnels, this one offers a gentle way
into a difficult land, cool melon, kif,
the soft bites of sleepy girls.
Bogart hesitates. A cat leaps down
through a shaft of sunlight, impossible
to tell its colour, black or white.

Remembers Bell on the boat, whetting
his blade through the night while everyone
slept off the desert like dogs.
*Kiss Kiss*, the brushing
of steel on stone. *Kiss Kiss*, dead centre
in a cave-dark night.

*So beat it pal I told you I've got other*
*fish to fry*, shoves a battered fist and its oily
package under the pointy, startled
nose: sardines from Seti, sea-perch and
eel for the bouillabaise.

## GUNDERSEN

Hated the boat at night, running for
smoky beaches, taking waves unseen from
behind, the hump and surge along the keel like a fat
snake swallowing.

Dreaded the weeds that combed along
legs and caught between toes, barbed and sudden things
that wiggled under sand or watched from the mind's weeds
for pierceable flesh.

No breeze that night or moon
or noise. Pushing to land in water warm as
blood you felt like an arm had floated off, a leg,
you'd clamp a hand to your groin to keep intact.
And then the fish, a tight-packed feeding bunch,
brushing thighs, boiling the water with fists
and tails like Brueghel's snouted hell, its
scaly tormentors with ragged teeth and pikes for
the latest arrivals. Gleeful, they dove to
puncture our groping, offending parts and drag us off
to worse below. And Gundersen broke for the background's
spit, bellowing, crawling on hands and knees
across the burning sea.

An hour we listened for wrong
sounds. The waves pushed past, lifting
us gently, letting us down. Side by side
like awkward boys in dancing class we tip-toed
forward and back again.

We found him wrecked in shells and weeds,
half-dead except for his eyes. They darted and
flashed in our careful light: what would he tell
Rashid? How would he deal with that white
theatrical eye? He knew what he'd lost and
the one way to find it—crawl back
to the water, grope with your
feet on the bottom.

# SMALL CAFE

*Sleepy cats*, murmurs Casselman, tugs
at the sleeve of our separateness drawing us down
to the smoky room. I clutch at the moon's corner,
wiggle it close to the window. I know this tone.
I want a quick way out. He's lounging under
the one thing hanging on the walls. Home,
you'd expect the hoisted Christ but here
it's blue-eyed Bobby Charlton, shoulder-high
in a cheering crowd. It's unambiguous winners
here go up on walls. There's little patience
with paradox, no gilded rules to grace
slack spirits. *Fat cats in the sun*, he says.
*You hardly see them here. Kittens everywhere but
never cats. You ever think about that?*

Outside the alley's ears are cocked.
Rashid is to come before morning.
Gundersen mutters, ill at ease with
tiny rooms and low tables. He's edgy, hates
the waiting, the games with Rashid and his wandering
eye. *Walls windows doors*—Casselman's said it
before, you lift the words like the edge of a tent.
What Gundersen wants is a flat field, morning's
frankness, battle skull to skull.

Slippers on the stairs, a slim hand
parts the beaded curtain, the owner's daughters
with candles and bowls: chicken, olives and lemon, *tajin*
with a meat of some sort. They lean across the table,
twist their spoons in steaming bowls, their movements
measured, revealing in the quarter-light an artful
curve of wrist. Casselman lifts his hands
in helpless pleasure, whispers to one then switches
to French to ask about their father and the ginger
cat, he hasn't seen either all week.

Bell sighs, pushes away his plate,
slips back from the light. The girls trap
giggles in nervous hands. *Kittens,* he says, tipping

the lid to sniff at the stew, *one of those
difficult words for men. Like cozy or tummy,
lover, brassiere. You ever think about
things like that?*

The face goes up through the low light
slowly, smoke from a bottle, the Viking body
follows, broad, menacing, brings to mind burning
towns, bloody flag-stones, women torn from corners.

The curse comes out of the dark, tells Casselman
what he can do with his thoughts, his cats
and cross-eyed friends. Then he steps,
like Gulliver, over the table, clumps down
a close and twisting stair-case meant
for a quicker people.

Casselman lifts an eyebrow, forks a chunk
of meat off Gundersen's plate.
*What's the matter?
Nobody hungry here?*

## PROVIDERS

Brushing flies from the limes,
barefoot, I start up the passage to see
what Bell's got for breakfast. Mussels, crab
would be good, mangos, drinking coconut milk
in the sun, closing deals for the world. But it's
rats on the step, tails carefully
curled, tiny grey toes.

I'm afraid to look up. I remember
a scuffling on deck in the night and old
Bogart slipped into my dreams, a battle-worn tom,
the only cat we could keep with a dairy
down the road. He scorned the dairy's
easy life, the laughable pounce of
milk-fat cats. He'd bring down rats,
rabbits and tangled once with a badger,
just to test his upper limits, my father figured.
Out in the fields we'd spot the tell-tale burst of
feathers or fur and left on the step a choice
bit of organ or leg he'd carried home.
Trophy or gift we never knew.
But who he'd brought it for we knew,
at least who'd find it first, racing out
to avert some other disaster, goats at the sheets
or hen-house trouble, my frazzled mother,
who never could learn to look
before she leapt.

*Casselman*, I murmur, *you remember
old Bogart*? Down in the gloom a groan,
a scruffling under the sheet. I glance up
at Bell in the hatch-way, grinning and
upside down. He sleeks down his hair with
the back of his hand, pleased with himself
and his artful arrangement.

I can't help wondering how they died.

## INVISIBLE MEN

That I needn't find four knees to know
both girls are on the bed asleep, three will do,
strikes me as absurdly clever. But what's become
of Bell? Smoke drifts in the dim room, curls, dips
to whisper praises at my ear, pleasing me immensely.
But only Bell can disappear. White as a wisp
and yellow hair you'd expect at least a glow.
But he's nowhere to be seen. Only his
voice in the room. Words without
end or beginning.

A tap spits.
The sly deceiver sniffs and,
departs, his mischief known—Bell's
in the bathroom: he talks through walls and
skulls, harries those other double-dealers,
memory and time. He straightens and tinkers and
trues: the Bad Map Trip, the Crippled Uncle
Debacle, Coca Cola Town, beamed and shuttered
rooms to wait out storms, old coats
for the wind like the rough-out
my father left in the barn until Fall.

A joke when Casselman and I were
kids: two invisible men talking, one says
*I guess you missed me when I was
gone.* The other asks him, startled,
*were you gone?*

My father turned left in October,
rode off to the mountains. Something about
the after-harvest light—he'd bend to the bales
in the morning gloom, but miles away you could see,
considering routes, seeing antlers scissor past
saplings. So here, a Moorish moon and sleepy girls
from Amsterdam. Something bunches under me: *hang on*
says carpet to the carpet rider. We float above
flat roofs and palms, off to the Atlas
and the morning's purple snow.

## YOUR OUTLINE ABOVE ME AS DARK AS THE NIGHT THEY CAME FOR YOUR FATHER

Better the way you wake me
in the night, no hammering doors, no fumbling
with housecoats. Nothing to fasten, a limp sheet,
your shoulder like a golden shell, an open
window to catch any breeze. Better the way you
talk behind my back, far better your whisper campaign,
the way you curl it across my neck. You plot my
descent. You murmur your dreadful intentions.
All my secrets you'll know—you take
my fingertips in your teeth until I
moan then slowly draw them down.
You push my shoulders down.
We sleep and wake and sleep again. Something
disturbs you under the window but no one comes
looking for trouble in shuffling *babouches*. I reach
for my glass in the dark. Your fingers brush down my
spine like a country girl crossing a brook, damp
woods all around: that week in Southern France,
walnuts in the wet grass stained our fingers
brown, the woods so still we listened to leaves
crashing down, here and here and there like a crowd
beginning to go, the home side done. Something starts
in undergrowth, a small panic, a twig and feather
battering, then silence. A rose-hip heart pumps
quickly. Sharply you draw your breath,
discovered. We creep together into
deeper cover, through carefully memorized tunnels.
We want box-hedge and ivy to crouch beneath, brambles,
hooked, deadly as hawk's-feet,
blood signs.

# GLASS CAT

After the desert, sleep's as coy as
a city cat. Under the cold moon or cramped
in the truck, nudged awake, I'd imagine these
moon-primed walls, the lovely sprawl of your
arms as you sleep, the blurred photograph of your
father on a favourite mare. Hard to see if he's
smiling or not—something's startled the mare or he's
trying to make her rear for the camera.

This from the movies and what your mother
remembers: mud they tracked inside, his bag
by the wall like a curled dog—*what a dog to sleep
through this.* And some I'd met, she said, sons of friends of
friends from Avignon—one night, not more, they'd see
to that. So why the fuss when he dressed, his shirt
and studs and collar just so—not to goad them as,
knowing him, you'd expect, but he'd seen Elise
behind the big glass cat. For her he'd
show his hands unshaken, proceeding at his own
good pace. I spoke in Arabic. He answered in
French—my language and theirs of course—in tenderness
or irony I never knew. Someone lied. Perhaps there were
other things I never knew. Well. Twenty years ago and
not more than twenty myself, not long from Marseille.
Odd how you expect so much. But still, I've bought
this small hotel and built the garden wall.
And set those lions at the gate.

Now you stretch like a fed cat to touch me
and settle again. Something about your
negligent perfection takes me back to the desert,
back to where, so certain once of friends, things
began to change, meetings not made, a cold look caught
by chance, a word expected undelivered.
And the doctor and his Arab mare—is this
the night's one theme? Close to the perfect
 gesture or moment, soldiers come, a careless
gun goes off or, thinking of something else,
someone takes the photograph too soon.

# ATROCITIES AND HOME TO LOVELY COUNTRIES

You're a terrible woman to take across
borders. Soldiers detain us at
check-points, road-blocks. In glossy
criss-cross belts with looping cords and
guns, the younger ones would make the search
inside. The older guards are doubters: who we are,
what we want, where we hide the bombs. They let
their flashlights linger on your knees.
They waggle significant forms.

But here it's ghosts who delay us,
the bleached bones of a post on the road to Rabat.
Acacias and vines reach over the wall. Reluctantly,
you slow to pass between the concrete prows,
softly cursing in Arabic the inconvenience
and the French

then swerve toward the snake
that darts across the road—you're
bent on murder here and all the troops have
gone, sent home by treaty or psychiatric decree
to a softer land, hunting birds in autumn fields,
tramping wet woods, knowing the grain is
safe and dry on the upper floor,
the lucky ones, home long enough
now to have doubled their herds and lives.

That leaves the snake and me. He's
quick and, wisely, lives beneath a solid wall.
But it's his bad luck the architects were
French. I see he nearly makes it home
but then the wall's too white and
large for me. I close my eyes.
I play no part in this. I've my own
atrocities to answer: Gordie Hogg for hauling down
my brother's pants and David Collins, exchanging
Christmas gifts in junior high, for him
*Johnny and the Hurricanes*, for me
a colouring book and crayons.

Then, unexpectedly, pavement again.
You pry my fingers from your thigh and
dare me with a sideways glance.
I see the leaves in the wipers
and think of how high your skirt's
ridden up in your anger and
shrug, content with a strange country
any Gordie Hogg or border guard would kill
to enter. Besides, I saw the snake's humiliating
death, writhing, snapping at air, no more than
half his length from home—I'm far
too far from my front door.

## DOG IN THE GLOOM

The edge of what abyss, Elise?
What dark wall do you tumble me down?
I reach for jutting stones. Windows slide past
in smoky light, troubled faces who reach
for me. One by one you pry my fingers
free and pull me down into
what world?  What things are these?—this gloom,
the dog with two heads too many, the still
pool where you wait. There's a face
in the water that blinks when I blink, turns
to you when I turn to you.

Why when I try to leave, this salty
odour of blood, this growling from dark
and close caves?  Animals wear my
faces, they leap to block my way.

# BACK AT MRS. LUND'S

Back in London we split up, shot-scattered
from a dry field. After the *khala's* raking
wind, the mist on my face like a
woman's breathing.

I sat under Nelson all day thinking
nothing. Tossing peanuts to pigeons.
Like a kid reading english on buildings
and circling busses: *Falstaff in
Open-Air, Short Lectures on Twain and
T. E. Lawrence.* KEEP GIBRALTER BRITISH!!!
And then the moonfaced girl with
circulars: *Ravel's Oiseaux Tristes.*

That night, I took the Underground
out to Mrs. Lund's. After the trucks
in rutted passes, this precise burrowing,
this blast into lit and certain destinations:
Covent Garden, Saint Pancras, Holloway Road,
Into the hole with the wolf at my heels. And Bell,
by the toss of a coin, turns in the bright sudden
square, his hands half-raised as if to say Okay Okay
I'll count to fifty you hide this time.

*Call you that backing of your friends?*

Past the Lebanese Bakery and Morrison's
Fish, the door stopped open with
the same stone. Past the corner
park with its few ducks.
The drizzle still.
*Oiseaux Tristes.*
The mist of her breath on my
wind-burnt face.

Behind her cigarette Mrs. Lund
blinks, turns on the stair to say I look
worse than ever and *where'd you get so
black then? Whose husband's after you now?*

The known smells. Boiled onions, damp
upholstery. *The Haywain* over a cluttered
mantle. The room unchanged except there's
lizards now—they're puzzled by the wallpaper's
faded hibiscus. One creeps too close to the heater's
coils. One slips and lands on my pillow,
a lump of plasticine.

*Lizards?* her left eye blinks and
locks. *We've never had lizards here—you've been
out in the sun too long.*

But even as she speaks, something's dark
behind her ear. Beneath her gypsy
bangle, the flick of an eye.

## CONSTABLE'S COWS

The flat light in the fields, hedge-rows,
comfortable cows, holsteins with little need now
for camouflage—anything wild left long ago
for the kept forests of fable. Someone's
crouched by the river but all he wants
is a stump to tie up his boat. For a moment
I forget the desert towns, the small, quick
things in corners. I lose myself in the reedy
landscape: a barge on the river bumps aside
rippling clouds, one cow turns to watch
the men on the opposite bank, the wagon
that close to the mill and sunk
to its bed in mud.

Weary or stubborn, the horses won't
budge. One of the men has started for
help. There's a barn behind the mill, a capable
horse at the half-door. A small dog by the mud-hole
bites at his leg, trying to make up his mind
to follow or stay and watch the fun.

But they're patient enough,
these squarish men who've stayed behind.
Hay-wagons get stuck when it's wet—what should
amaze about that? They've kicked the flat
stones firmly into place and heave
together on the pry. They'll likely be
late for dinner again but after a difficult day
night arrivals have their own deliciousness.

Native and predictable disasters.
A muddy road, a poor price for grain at
one end, a sulky wife at the other.
Without such certainties what would
life be? The face of the fourth
you can't quite see. He doesn't
look back, never doubting the others
will still be there when he returns, mud
past their knees, locked in the dangerous
angle of their leaning.

# CHINA DUCKS

> *Faith, I ran when I saw others run.*
> *Henry IV (pt. one).*

91 Orchard Lane, Finsbury Park, the sky
dull as an old spoon. A dray
disturbs my sleep—dropping something
or collecting? The broad back strapped and
steaming, a good place for boys in winter or
trouble. Swing up from the manger.
Stretch out in the gloom of beams.
This one clunks a shoe against the curb
to mention oats. What treachery's here,
I wonder half-awake, then slide into sleep
again: desert horses don't need shoes.

Mrs. Lund is cross, feeling thwarted. Clumps
to the window, lets in a spiteful murder novel's
mist. Why won't I talk she wants to know.
Why won't I come at night for tea?
She wants me up and out for air—I've
had enough of open space and air.

*Hey Casselman!*
*Remember when Old McCambridge*
*came after us? We'd bet poor Lily wouldn't*
*lick the 40 gallon drum? Dead of winter, 20 below.*
*Lucky I had the rack and team—we drove her*
*straight into the barn, still stuck to the rim.*
*She couldn't talk until spring.*

Now my own tongue's thick with silence.

Sounds of fussing around me.
Pairing shoes. Dusting china ducks.
Not enough to deal with, now this change
of air in the room. I crawl deeper under
the covers and grope for my dream.
This one I want to finish.